T0209029

THE DEREK KENISTON STORY

Who Am I...

Tim Keniston

WESTBOW
PRESS®
A DIVISION OF THOMAS NELSON
& ZONDERVAN

WestBow Press books may be ordered through booksellers or by contacting:

WestBow Press
A Division of Thomas Nelson & Zondervan
1663 Liberty Drive
Bloomington, IN 47403
www.westbowpress.com
1 (866) 928-1240

ISBN: 978-1-5127-1289-6 (sc)
ISBN: 978-1-5127-1290-2 (e)

Library of Congress Control Number: 2015915137

Print information available on the last page.

WestBow Press rev. date: 09/23/2015

Dedication

This book is lovingly dedicated to the memory of Derek Keniston......
A Loving Son, Brother, and Friend. Also to all the people who
walked this journey with us.

Be strong and courageous.

Do not be afraid or terrified

b**E**cause of them, for the LORD

you**R** God goes with you; he will

n**E**ver leave you nor

forsa**K**e you.

Deuteronomy 31:6

This was Derek's favorite verse that he clung to during this battle. For we all have victory in JESUS.

THE PURPOSE
OF THIS BOOK

About two years after Derek passed away, I was awakened by God as He was talking to my heart about the last couple of years. If I'm being honest with you, those were two of the hardest years of my life. I don't remember much. I guess I was just too numb with so much heartache. Each day was just a struggle to get up and function. So as the Father was revealing all of the things that He did during and after our journey that we were on with Derek. He told me "Tim, I'm going to make you a fisher of men and not a bass fisherman anymore. I want you to go tell my story of my love for my children even when sometimes we have to go through deep valleys and sorrow."

For three nights He burned this story into my heart. As He showed me what all He wanted me to tell, one of the first things I said was "Me?" I had taught Sunday school at my Church, but I had never spoke before groups of people, and of course God told me "I can to all things through Christ Who strengthens me. I will be with you."I have put it on paper the way He outlined it in my heart, and I kind of started rehearsing it in my head, and God would make small changes, and sometimes He would wake me up in the night so I would go write it down. After having it the way He wanted it. It was not too long after that, I got asked to speak at a men's meeting. After that I started getting asked to speak at other engagements and I continue to say "yes Lord".

The Bible tells us, All Things Work for His Glory "Jesus" and the little word "All" just doesn't mean good. Sometimes there are bad things that happen, but yet God allows them to happen to do what He needs to accomplish.

Sometimes He even has to tell us "No" to allow what He wants to accomplish. The hard part in all of this as Christians is when he says "No." I struggled with this because the Bible says "The Fervent Prayer of a Righteous Man Eveleth Much." James 5:16 because we had hundreds of righteous men and women praying for Derek's healing. Because the last verse of John says. "I suppose if all of the miracle's and other things that Jesus did were recorded in books, the world it's self could not contain them all." John 21:25

As I was dealing with all of this, the Father told me "Tim I had to tell my own Son no the night before in the garden." Then I began to understand just how much our Father God truly loves us. Even when he tells us no, and it hurts so much. He is doing all things for His Glory.

The purpose of this book is to tell of God's love and to encourage people when we are going through very difficult times that the Great I AM is with us always. And I just don't want people to remember that Tim and Lisa lost a son to Cancer. I want people to remember how perfect God was and all of the miracle's He did through and after the event and how much He loves us.

My prayer is that it helps someone else along the way. In Jesus Name Amen.

THE NEWS

Labor Day weekend 2009 like a lot of families, we were looking forward to a three day weekend. Filled with cook outs, fishing, football, and just family time. I had taken off work early at noon to get the mowing done so it would be out of the way. Lisa was taking off early to go by the store to pick up food for the cookouts and items we would need to go fishing out on the boat.

Derek our 19 year old son, who had just started his sophomore year at college had just gotten out of class around noon and decided to stop at the clinic to see if he could get in and have his hamstring checked, because it was hurting him real bad and had been for some time.

Derek had a part time job as a little league umpire, and had jumped out of the way of a foul ball and he had thought he had re-aggravated an old hamstring injury from football. Derek had been to the Doctor a couple of times already to have it checked and it just was not getting any better. So when he got in to see the Doctor, he explained what was going on with his leg and also mentioned there was a lump on his abdomen and he asked the doctor to look at it too. The Doctor wanted to put his mind at ease so he said as small as Derek was he could use an ultra sound machine to see what was going on inside, and ordered an ultra sound to be done. In the middle of the Ultra sound the technician got up and went and got the doctor. They had found something that did not belong there.

The Doctor told us that they found a large mass on his spleen, and he would have to have immediate surgery to remove it. He had already gotten in contact with a surgeon who specialized in this type of surgery. Because of it being Labor Day weekend none of the Doctors would be able to do anything until Tuesday.

That Sunday morning Derek and his girlfriend went down and talked to the Pastor and told him what was going on and asked him to pray for him. The rest of us went down to the altar and prayed for Derek, and for healing.

Tuesday morning we were at the Surgeon's office at 9 a.m. The Doctor examined Derek, looked at the ultra sound imaging and confirmed that there was a mass that did not belong and was going to send Derek over to the hospital for a couple of more tests and would be back at his office at 3 p.m. that day. When we got back to his office, he told us that our son needed immediate surgery, and there was a mass around the spleen that needed to come out, and that he would have to remove the spleen also. Derek was scheduled for surgery the following Monday due to the Doctor's schedule and more tests needing to be done.

Surgery day comes and the plan was to go in arthroscopically and break up the tumor with tiny incisions and as they got in they realized the tumor was larger than they first thought, and Derek would have to be opened up to remove the tumor and spleen. When the surgery was over the Doctor came to us and told us that the tumor was the size of a football and weighed about 8lbs. He said it was an angry tumor, and that nobody in the hospital could identify it and they would have to send it off for testing. Derek would be in the hospital for at least 5 days for recovery. During that time they also did pet scans on his body to see if there were any other masses. That Friday we found out that he had cancer spots that showed up behind one knee, the leg that was hurting so much, his hip and there was a mass between the kidney and bladder that could not be operated on. They told us that the type of cancer Derek had was called Angio Sarcoma. A very rare cancer which not much is known about and that they would get us in touch with an Oncologist to help us with a treatment plan.

They sent Derek home and said he had to rest and heal from his surgery for a few weeks, and then they would be in touch with the oncologist to have an action plan for when he was well enough to undergo treatment. Derek was given the option of going to MD Anderson or staying local with a Doctor here who could do the same treatments. Surgery was out of the question on tumors on hip and knees and the tumor between his kidney and bladder. Derek decided to stay local and undergo treatment where he could still be close to home, family and friends. We were told Derek's cancer was stage 4 and he would have to undergo chemotherapy and radiation. (What was a healthy son one day, was stage 4 cancer and a fight for his life within two weeks.)

We met our Oncologist and staff and he told us he would start treatment with four types of chemo every third week and radiation everyday over the course of several months, and so we began.

THE FIGHT BEGINS

Before Derek could start the treatment. He had to have minor surgery to have a port put in to be able to get the Chemo because it was too strong to go into arm veins. He also had to have a stress test to check to see if his heart was strong enough to handle the amount of chemo they were going to have to put into him.

On Monday morning the first week of October Derek went in to start his regiment of treatments. Monday would consist of 2 types of Chemo drugs which would last all day long and then we would go for radiation for an hour and a half and on Monday nights we had to bring chemo medicine home and an Ivy bag full of medicines to protect his kidneys from the chemo.

Tuesdays we had to be back at the Oncologist by 7am to start 2 more kinds of chemo and other medications to keep the body from breaking down too much. When we were done there, Derek had to be taken over to another clinic for radiation treatments.

Wednesday we were back at the Oncologist for one more type of chemo and replenishment fluids and when all of that was done, we headed back over to the clinic for radiation treatment.

Thursday we were back at Oncologist for blood work, Ivy fluids, shots, and all this was to help with chemo that was given earlier in week and to check his blood counts. Then back to radiation clinic for an hour and a half.

Fridays would consist of stopping by the Oncologist to do more blood work and then back over for radiation.

The next week we would have to watch Derek and they would have to check and monitor his blood cell counts and platelets but he would still go for radiation daily. At times he would have to have blood transfusions or platelets, depending on what his counts were.

The third week was Derek's rest week. He would have to build up his strength to start over the following week with chemo again. But the radiation would continue. So every day we were at one of three clinics getting something done. Derek never complained through it all, even though it made him very sick and weak.

The next three months, October, November, and December this was our routine. In the month of December complications from the cancer pain and not being able to eat, all started to take its toll on Derek. I will tell more about December as I tell about God's miracle's later in the book.

January comes around with treatments starting over and treatments continued through March. In April they did a pet scan and the cancer hot spots are not lighting up or what they called hot spots, and so for the months of May and June and the first half of July, Derek had no treatments because we were told Derek's cancer was in remission.

For the months of May, June and July. Derek was feeling well enough to go back to work full time, and we got as much family time and fishing time as possible. Derek almost feels like his old self again. Late July, Derek starts feeling bad again and he has another pet scan. The cancer has returned with a vengeance. It is in his liver, lungs, and thymus. They want to do one massive dose of Chemo again to try and stop the cancer. But the decision is up to Derek. And he decides to go ahead with their plan. They tell me and his mom, Derek probably has around 90 days left.

On October 7th 2010 at 4:35 a.m. after fighting like a Champion and never complaining, Derek goes home to be with his Lord.

THIS STORY DOES NOT END HERE. GOD DOES SO MANY THINGS PERFECTLY WITH MIRACLES AND HE SHOWS US HIS LOVE THROUGH IT ALL.

CHAPTER 3

THE LAY OFF

In the month of December 2009 Derek was in the hospital. His pain was very high and oral pain medication was no longer working. He was also getting weaker, and was unable to even stand on his own. While we were there I get a phone call from a co-worker telling me we all just got laid off, and that the company was closing their doors. At first I was in shock and could not believe what I was hearing. I thought this cannot be happening, but then I realized God was in control. You are wondering why a lay off would be considered a Miracle? For you see Derek had gotten weaker and was not doing very good. One of us, either mom or dad was going to have to take a leave of absence from work, to help get Derek back and forth for all of his treatments. The natural choice was dad because he was able to get him in and out of the vehicle and help him get into the restrooms. The insurance was through moms work and so she needed to keep working to be able to keep Derek on her insurance, but we were ultimately going to lose an income. So God steps in and works it out perfectly. By letting me get laid off, so I was able to draw unemployment benefits and still help Derek full time, and spend precious time with my son. So here is God being perfect with a situation that we had no control over, and yet God works it out in perfect timing.

THE CHRISTMAS MIRACLE

The second week in December 2009 Derek entered the hospital. Almost unable to walk due to the cancer in his bones and affecting the nerves in his lower body. He was not eating and was getting weaker. So they admitted him into the hospital to try and get his pain under control and to get his nausea under control so he could start eating again. Derek was in the Hospital for about two and a half weeks while they tried several types of medications which none worked very well. At this point he is very weak and almost ready to give up. The Doctor said we have one last option and he was going to get ahold of a pain specialist to see what they thought could be done.

After visiting with the pain specialist. We decided to try what they were suggesting, which was to put a pain pump in his abdomen with a lead that would run under the skin and into the nerves of the spinal cord in his lower back. We took Derek over to the Pain management hospital for them to do a trial pain pump to see if it would work and if it did then they would put in a permanent one. This was on the 21st day of December. It worked like they hoped it would, and started helping with the pain. So the

Doctor said this was just a test to see if it would work and the real one would work a whole lot better than even this.

They scheduled surgery on December 23rd to install the permanent pain pump which was the size of a hockey puck, in the left side of Derek's lower abdomen just underneath the skin, which held a concentrated form of pain medication that automatically dispensed medication at certain time intervals directly into the nerves in the back to block the pain. With the help of a Specialist from the company that makes them. He and the pain Doctor installed the pain pump. They had told us that there could be complications, infections, both in spine and in the abdomen and or the body could reject the device under the skin. If it worked and everything went well, Derek would get immediate relief and be virtually pain free. So God steps in and lets everything go perfectly. No infections, no complications, and on Christmas Eve, Derek walks out of the hospital, not in a wheel chair, not with a walker, he walks out of the hospital on his own and we go home.

When we get to the house and as he is walking in the door, Derek said "I'm hungry, when is the Ham and Turkey going to be ready?"

That night on Christmas Eve night, God allows the most beautiful 8 inch snow to fall so when we woke up on Christmas morning we had a White Christmas. Everyone knows, there is just something about dreaming of a White Christmas. So here is our Father God, giving us a beautiful, perfect, pain free, White Christmas with our son. At the time, we did not know it would be our last Christmas with our son. But God knew that it was, and he made it beautiful.

CHAPTER 5

CATCH A DREAM TRIP
TO LAKE FALCON

In February 2010 as Derek was getting stronger with the pain pump working and being able to take Chemo and Radiation treatments again. One of Derek's High school teachers Debbie got in contact with The Catch a Dream Foundation, about offering Derek a fishing trip of a lifetime. I guess I should have told you all from the beginning that Derek loved to fish. Ever since he was a little boy, Derek dreamed of being a Professional Fisherman. So we were on the water as much we could be, as time would allow as he was growing up.

When Catch a Dream contacted us and was offering Derek this trip, Derek said he wanted to go to Lake Falcon and fish with his fishing hero Edwin Evers. Edwin is a Bass Pro Shop Pro and fishes the Bass Master Elite Series. You see Edwin had come by our home in October in 2009 to meet Derek. Derek had had a bad week of Chemo and was not feeling very well and when the doorbell rang, I told Derek to answer the door and that it was for him. He said dad I really don't feel like it. I said you really need to answer the door.

When Derek opened the door, his fishing hero, Edwin Evers was standing there. Feeling bad from all of the chemo kind of went away. For the next 2 and a half hours Edwin and Derek visited and hit it off like old friends. But one of the questions Edwin asked Derek was, if you died today do you know where you would go. Do you know that you know? Derek said yes I know where I would go. I am a Christian and I am saved. Derek asked if his best friend Tyler could come over and meet him too, because Edwin was his fishing hero too. So Derek, Tyler and Edwin talked fishing for another hour and just visited. From that point on Edwin stayed in contact with Derek and would visit him several times in the Hospital and call on the phone when he was on the road at a tournament. Edwin even took him fishing just him and Derek a month before Derek passed away.

Back to the Lake Falcon Fishing trip. We were trying to figure out dates that would work with the Chemo and radiation treatments and the time that would work out with Edwin on his busy schedule. The week of February 14th, 15th and 16th was the dates that Edwin could go and would work for us as well. The trip was scheduled and everything with Derek had to go perfectly, with him having Chemo the week before and all of his blood counts had to be good for him to be able to make the trip. So here is God stepping in 2 ways. First letting Derek be health enough and not needing blood transfusions, or platelets or anything else going wrong to be able to make the trip. God let everything go smoothly for him to be able to make the trip to Lake Falcon in Zapata, Texas. The second thing that God did was (here is where it gets interesting) you see I had shared with you about Edwin Evers. For a Pro Fishermen, the Bassmaster Classic is the biggest event of there year. In 2009 everything that could go wrong Edwin will tell you, cost him from making the classic in February of 2010 the same time we were taking our trip to Lake Falcon. Before we ever knew Derek had Cancer, here is God working on Edwin's life and our lives at the same time, a year in advance, and we did not even know it to make this trip happen. Edwin has never not qualified for the Bassmaster Classic before that year or since that year. He will tell you he firmly believes it all happened because he was supposed to be at Lake Falcon fishing with Derek.

We headed out on our trip on February 14th and it was snowing at the airport when we were leaving. Derek and Daren had never been on a plane before. We were also able to take Derek's older brother David too. He was flying from New York and meeting up with us in Dallas, then we all boarded a plane that took us to South Texas where we would meet our host Kevin Drewry with the Catch a Dream Foundation. We drove to Zapata, Texas where we were to stay for the next few days. That evening we met up with Edwin and the Guides that would be taking us fishing at Lake Falcon. We all went out to dinner that night and the next morning the fishing trip began. Derek and Edwin fishing side by side. Laughing, catching fish, and telling stories. Derek got to do what he had always dreamed of. Fishing with Edwin on Lake Falcon a lake he had only dreamed about fishing.

Our Father God causes all of this to come about without Derek being sick after Chemo treatment, and Edwin getting to spend time off the circuit to fish with him. In a way the whole trip was a much needed break for the whole family. And everyone caught fish, and Derek caught a hog, and had a great time.

We want to thank our guides who were so kind, Jim, Louigy, Jim, and the town of Zapata who made us all feel so welcome while we were there. Kevin Drewry with the Catch a Dream Foundation. Who are all in our eyes, first class people! So if you think about all of the events of this story and how it all came together, there is only one conclusion, we have an Awesome God.

THE VISION AT CHURCH

What I am about to share with you happened 2 weeks after Derek went home to be with the Lord. It happened at our Church where we have been members for several years. All I can do is try to put into words what the Lord did as he started restoring and healing my heart.

We were standing as the Praise and Worship Service started and I have to tell you, there was not much joy in my heart. As hard as I tried, I could not get my lips to sing to one of my favorite songs. I had tears running down my cheeks as I was trying to worship my Savior. All of a sudden, my eyes go blind, and I see a vision of Derek standing in a Choir and he is singing the same song as we are singing, with a huge smile on his face. He is wearing a shirt that he did not own, he was well and did not look like he had ever had cancer. Here is the funny thing about that. Derek never sang in a choir because he did not have the best vocal voice. The only time he ever sang is when he was driving down the road and all the windows were rolled up, by himself.

I hear a voice whisper in my ear, "see Tim, I told you he is alright." And at that moment my eyes were focused back to what was going on in my Church, and a smile came upon my face and my lips were able to start singing again. I believe this was God starting the healing in my heart and putting a little joy in my soul that day.

DEREK'S MISSING KEYS

After Derek's cancer had went into remission and he had started going back to work full time he had decided he wanted a pickup. He believed his cancer was gone. He found a black truck, but the dealership said he would have to have a co-signer. He went to his mom and asked her for help. His mom's heart melted and she agreed to sign the papers.

At some point during that month Lisa was teasing Derek and said since she had co-signed for the truck then she gets to drive it too. The look on his face was priceless, at that point Derek runs to where the extra set of keys were hanging and takes off to his room with them to hide them. We all busted out laughing.

After Derek had passed away we needed the extra set of keys. We had forgotten all about Derek hiding them. Lisa looked for them on and off for several days and then she gave up. Deciding that we really did not need them that bad.

About a month later she was getting ready for work sitting at the kitchen table putting on makeup, and she heard a soft voice say "the keys are in my hunting bag". She was running late for work so she ignored it, but thought about looking for them again later, and did not think much more about it. The next morning she was at the kitchen table again putting on her makeup. She heard Derek's voice again say "Mom, the keys are in the front pocket of my hunting bag". Lisa immediately stopped and ran to his room and opened his closet door and looked down at his hunting bag and knew this was not a coincidence, she really heard him. She bent down and slowly, unzipped the front pocket and reached in and pulled out the extra set of keys to Derek's truck. She busted out laughing with joy that God allowed Derek to contact her in such a way that she had no doubt it was him.

THE DREAM

One night about three weeks after Derek had gone home to be with the Lord. I was trying somehow to get sleep. Trying to shut my mind off from all of the events that had taken place over the last few weeks. One of the things that had bothered me so much, was that I was unable to tell Derek goodbye and tell him all of the things I had tried so hard to do for him while he was sick. Derek got sick really fast at the very end. I longed for him to know I had spent hours on my knees begging God to put it in me and let him live, because he had so much to look forward to. So much he had not gotten to experience. I would have gladly taken his place if God would have allowed it.

I also kept having flash backs of when I had found out that the cancer was back and I kept it from him for 48 hours not wanting to ruin his weekend, or wanting him to know how bad it really was, because he had just started to enjoy things again, and started going out with friends. Or the time me and him had went fishing and because of the steroids he was taking he had gotten angry with me and I regretted causing him to get angry with me while we were doing something we loved together.

I had just fallen asleep, when I started having a dream and Derek walked up to me in the dream with a big smile on his face. He puts his arms around me and gives me a big Derek hug, kisses me on the cheek (and I can still feel the kiss today) and he says "Dad, thank you for all you did for me. I love you. I have to go now." I watched him walk into the most beautiful light I have ever seen. Then he was gone.

There is no doubt in my mind God knew what I needed to hear from my son and he let Derek come to me to help with the healing of my heart.

Thank You Lord.

CHAPTER 9

THE VIDEO

About a week before the one year anniversary of Derek's passing, we get a phone call from Edwin Evers. He is wanting to do a fishing tribute video about Derek and wanting it to air on the fishing channel. We get everything planned and the video was going to be with Derek's younger brother Daren, Derek's best friend Tyler, and Edwin. We are going to go to Lake Spavinaw which was Derek's favorite lake. We had spent a lot of time there when Derek was younger and had caught a lot of bass there.

The morning of October 7th 2011 we all met to start the filming of the show. Which was the one year anniversary of Derek's passing. I believe this was by God's design so that it helped a really hard day maybe get a little bit easier in the hearts of a dad, brother, and friends. For the next couple of days the guy's fish together, tell stories, and remember our son Derek.

While they were on the water, Edwin allowed Derek's younger brother Daren to drive his Pro Fishing Boat, and we all could picture Derek up in heaven jealous as can be, over his little brother getting to drive his hero's boat.

When the video came out and was on TV, they had taken a clip from our trip to Lake Falcon and put it into the video for the opening scene. It was Derek and Edwin fishing side by side. What was cool, was Derek had always dreamed of being on TV fishing like a pro. Here he was on TV on the Bass channel catching a bass.

I know that Tyler and Daren really enjoyed getting to spend time together and fishing with Edwin and reminiscing about Derek. I believe somehow Derek was there in spirit along with them.

About a year after this Edwin was fishing the All Star Classic and was asked about the emblem on his boat that read (In Loving Memory Derek Keniston 1990-2010) and has a bass emblem in the middle of it. The story the 13th All Star was written in the fishing magazine about Derek and his courage. Edwin tells his story about how Derek touched his life, and it tells each one of us how precious each day, life is.

CHAPTER 10

THE BLESSING
IN OUR DOOR

First I need to explain a little bit about what was going on. Due to the extensive amount of Medical bills and getting laid off during Derek's illness and only getting unemployment benefits and then having difficulty going back into the work force after losing my son, the bills had piled up. We had been behind on a lot of bills. We did not know what to do and we were deciding on if we really wanted to stay in our house with all that had happened. With all the memories of Derek's last month's here. Our home was in foreclosure, and fixing to be put up for auction in the next two weeks, because we were several months behind on our house payments and a couple of months behind on our car payments.

While all of this was going on I had just gotten a job that would have allowed us to make the house payments again. I had been talking with the mortgage company and had let them know that I had a job where we felt like we could make a house payment again and not knowing what to do because we were so far behind. And then!

I got a call from my 15yr old son Daren who had just gotten home from school and had just walked up to our front door and when he opened the screen door to come in there was an envelope laying in the door with $9000 dollars in 100 dollar bills and he says Dad, were you expecting a large amount of money today? I said no, why? He tells me about the money he found in an unmarked envelope in the front door, with a note inside that read "already been tithed and taxed." Daren said, "Dad, I'm scared being here alone with all this cash." So I went to my boss and explained what had happened and left to go get the money and put it in the bank. We were over whelmed with thankfulness to God and who ever had blessed us with this great need. This confirmed in our hearts that we should stay here in our home.

The next day I got ahold of the mortgage company and let them know that we could get caught up and be able to make our payments again if we could keep the house. As I was talking with them they started working on their end, on the options that we had, and he said he would call back the next day. When he called back they told us what they would do. Our interest rate would go from 7.9% to 3.5% and we would refinance and our new house payment would go down and be what we could live with. So we mailed a check the next day with the amount they needed, and all foreclosures stopped, and the auction that was scheduled for that weekend was canceled. We also had enough money to get caught up on my wife's car payments and the 2 truck payments that we were behind on. What I should also share with you is we had not packed a box, not even been looking or getting ready to move before this had happened.

I believe our God who is perfect, our God who loves, had all of this worked out ahead of time, as only He can. God knew exactly to the penny how much money was needed to get us back on track. And to the person or persons who blessed us by placing the money in our front door. May God Bless You 10 fold for your gift of love.

CHAPTER 11

LIVES TOUCHED

Three years after Derek's passing a couple of girls came up to my wife in a grocery store and said "Mrs. Keniston? We have been wanting to tell you this, but didn't know when the right time was. We knew Derek from school, and we just wanted you to know we had went to his funeral and after hearing the Preacher talk about Derek and his faith, and how strong he was, knowing he would ultimately be with Christ. We were touched. When they asked if anyone would like to talk to someone, and find out more about Jesus, or if they had questions, there would be people to talk to after the service." They said "we wanted to know that kind of peace and love. Mrs. Keniston, we just wanted you to know we are now Christians and go to Church faithfully and are active in our Church and our husbands and children go too."

My wife hugged them both and told them thank you for telling her this, and that she was so happy for them all. So here is our Father God, three years after the fact, confirming in our hearts and letting us know that he is still at work in other people's lives, and in our lives, because of Derek's story.

CHAPTER 12

JASON'S STORY

As we share this story with you, think of all of the parts of it and how it affected so many lives and how it came together in perfect timing. Where there is no doubt about it. It is God at work.

On a Saturday morning in October, 2 months into Derek's fight with cancer and he had a hard week of chemo and radiation. I get a phone call and the voice on the other end says, "Hi I'm Jason Keniston your cousin. You don't know me, but I saw on Facebook that my cousin has cancer. I have driven all night from Michigan to see him. Would it be alright if I came over to visit? I have been in town trying to find out where you all live and someone gave me your phone number and that is why I am calling."

I need to explain something. The reason that I did not know about Jason is, his dad and my dad are twin brothers. My dad died 25 years ago and not knowing my dad's brother very well and the fact that he lived so far away. I did not know he had a young son that was the same age 19, as Derek.

Back to the phone call. I go and meet Jason in town and bring him out to our home to meet the family. It turns out that Jason and Derek had like interests, both played high school football, ran track, were in College and perhaps would become Teachers. Both very athletic and competitive.

Derek was not feeling well that weekend because of the chemo and radiation but it seemed to help Derek for Jason to be there. Having Jason here and being able to talk sports and visit, for the weekend they hung out playing cards, watching football, and telling stories of their own high school football and track glory days.

As we all got to know Jason, we found out that he had the same birthday as my sister Tonya. We talked about his family and the plans that he had. I could just tell there was something different about this young man. How many nineteen year olds would take the incentive to drive all night long to come and see a family that he had never met until now? I believe it was nothing short of God starting a work in his life. Because Jason had not been raised in a Christian home or environment. After a good weekend visit, Monday comes and as we are headed off for Derek to go to the Doctors and Jason to go back home to Michigan. God tells me to tell Jason "He has Great Things in Store for Him." And that is exactly what came out of my mouth before I even knew it. Jason looked at me and he said, "Tim I want what you all have" and I said Jason you don't want what we are going through right now. Jason replied back "no, I mean the God thing. It's just different here. You guys just have a peace about you, even with all the heartache that is going on right now." I replied back, listen to your heart and God will show you what to do.

As I look back now. I probably should have said more, but we were all fixing to leave, and there was no time. But I know now it was not God's timing yet, and I will explain more a little later on why.

We kept in touch through texts, Facebook and phone calls over the next several months and Jason's plans were to come back that summer to visit again. In the meantime Jason had gotten a job and was unable to come back that summer. Derek's cancer had went into remission that summer also, and he was doing better. So everything did not come together for Jason to come back. Again as I tell this story you will see God's perfect timing.

On a Thursday morning October 7th 2010 at 4:35 a.m. Derek went home to be with the Lord. I sent out a text to everyone that said "Derek had gone home." Jason was walking to class in Michigan when he received my text about 8:00 a.m. In the morning.

If you look at the time difference there is a time lapse between when I sent the text and when Jason received it. And yes there is an hour difference in time, but not 3 and a half hours between here and there. Jason was just about to enter class and after seeing the text he started crying and he asked his professor if he could be excused from class and he left. Jason started walking off campus, and started walking down the street, he is talking to God, crying and not understanding all that has happened. He sat down on some steps and puts his head in his hands and sobs. He feels a hand on his shoulder and he looks up and the man says. "Son are you ok?" Jason responds back and says, "No sir, I am not. I am so confused, and I just don't understand all that has happened." As Jason starts to explain all that has happened, the man says. "I happen to be the Pastor of the Church you are sitting in front of. Would you like to go inside and talk?" Until that moment, Jason did not even realize he had been sitting in front of a Church. When they get inside the Pastor said "do you believe that the God that created everything and has brought me and you here to this Church together today, when today was my day off, and I had forgotten the book that I needed to prepare my lesson, and came back to get it, was meant for a purpose, or just a coincidence?" and Jason said "I don't believe this is a coincidence." So he and Jason went into the Pastor's office. Jason prayed and accepted Christ that day. After they visited Jason asked if he could stay in the chapel for a while and he picked up the Bible and read the book of John. Where the Pastor had told him to read.

As I am sharing this with you, I hope you realize that on my darkest day, God was furthering the Kingdom for His glory. As one soul was going home, another soul was being saved.

The story just doesn't end here. Jason, a new Christian, the following summer enlists in the Army Reserves to help pay for college. While he is at training camp. He witnesses to several of the young men there with him. God uses him to lead four men to the Lord, and he and the Chaplin baptize 20 men that summer. They made the baptismal out of tarps and filled them full of water. Jason said that he would just share Derek's story, and then his story with them, and the Love of Christ.

Here is more to the story. When Jason started school the next fall, he transferred to Malone Christian University. While he was there, he was sharing Derek's story with whomever would listen. One day I get a call from him and he has asked his Professor if I could share Via Phone with the class about Derek's Story. I was able to do a phone conference with the class.

Jason also wanted to have a Christian concert at Malone, so he started to work on it. He wanted Christian artists their and also to do a food drive along with it. Jason was able to get several big Christian artist there. Also they were able to do the food drive to benefit hungry children in the area. Jason was able to share his personal testimony with the lead singer of one of the groups. The lead singer for Building 429 wrote Derek's name on his hand that he holds the mike with and you could see it as he sang. He also at the end of the concert asked everyone to be quiet and he turned down the lights and as they sang there song of the year, (This is Not My Home) he said. "This one's for Derek."

I know we will probably never know all of the people that this one young man has impacted for Christ. As I share the last part of Jason's story with you. He too had an impact on my life. In the first few months after Derek died. One night I was outside crying and I was asking God why. I was hurting and was so sad and not much seemed to make much sense at that moment. The phone rings and it is Jason. He tells me that the Holy Spirit told him to call me. Jason did not know why he was supposed to call until he got me on the phone and I had shared with him how badly I was hurting that night. I told him I felt like Derek's death was in vain. And then Jason told me if it wasn't for Derek and our story and our lives, that he would not have been saved. He reminded me of how it all came to pass, that he Jason was saved and how his life had been changed forever. And this reminded me of the Father's love and how sometimes he has to say no, to accomplish what he needs to do. So you can look back on Jason's story and see God's perfect timing, His Perfect Love, and all the things that He did, and is still doing to this day with Jason and us!

CHAPTER 13

LOOKING BACK

Derek's brothers and friends want people to remember

Derek's older brother David wanted to say how he felt about his brother in a letter to him.

> Dear Derek,
>
> I am eternally grateful for every day that I knew you. I wish every day that we could have had more. I remember the day you were born like yesterday. I remember learning the emotion of pride as I held you in my arms. I also remember our last days together. They were the most difficult of my life. But I try to remember the days in between above all else.
>
> You blessed my life in ways I could never put into words. The way you smiled at me like we knew something that no one else could. And we did. That special connection is what I miss the most.
>
> I know you are in a far better place now, and you will always live on through the lives of the

countless others you blessed. It has truly been
one of my biggest life honors to call you my
brother. I love you with all of my heart.

-David

What Derek's younger brother Daren wants people to know about his brother. "The most important life lesson I learned from my brother through his life was to never give up. It sounds cliché but it is true. Every picture, every memory, every glimpse I see of my brother, he has his chest stuck out and his head held high.

Yes there were moments he was weak, but he tried so hard not to show it. It wasn't because he was too proud or didn't want people to worry. Derek knew something most of us take a lifetime to realize.

My brother understood that he was God's creation and no matter what, he was perfect. Through the sickness, and everything, my brother knew that God saw him as perfect and had a plan. He accepted that his life would end early better than anyone I have ever seen, and it was because he knew God's purpose is greater than anything he could have done on his own.

So the lesson I hope everyone remembers is to not give up. Even if the end is near. Understand that even in the last moments of your life, God is using you to help or save someone else."

Derek's best friend Tyler said, one of my fondest memories of Derek was a trip to Chelsea Lake. We were there doing some night fishing in an old small 2 man boat, that had been given to him by his grandpa, and when we got there, we had no idea there was a hole in the scamp until we had fished for a couple of hours, when we noticed water was coming up thru the bottom of the boat and he looked over at me and said "I believe we have a hole in the bottom of the boat" and I said "I believe your right." We were about 2 hundred yards from the boat ramp and needed to get back to it. When we finally arrived at the boat ramp we could not get the scamp out of the water because it was so heavy and full of water. We finally found out where the hole was, there was a crack along the whole length of the boat on one side. So we, being the diehard fishermen that we were, we decided we could still fish, if we kept leaning on the other side of the boat while fishing and keep the crack out of the water. We fished for several more hours and we caught some really big bass. But as for the scamp, that was its last day on the water.

There was one more time when we almost sunk his Bass boat that he had just gotten. We went to a fishing tournament on Lake Hudson and it was so windy and the waves were big and we hit a wave that engulfed the boat and completely filled it with water because Derek did not know we should have not put the boat on plane trying to go across the lake. I got drenched and thought we were going to die or sink the boat. Derek kept saying we were going to be ok, we got to shore and Derek was just as calm as can be.

These two stories are just a few of the many adventures we experienced together. He was my best friend and through all of our time together he taught me to keep faith and never give up, and he would say during his time when he was so sick "It's not how you die, it's how you live" and he lived.....3 years later after Derek's death, I met my beautiful wife and we got married, We just recently had a baby boy (my new fishing buddy) and I have named him after Derek in memory of my forever friend.

Derek's other close friend Bobby said "I have thought about him every day and I don't know how to put my memories of Derek on paper. He is simply the greatest person I know and always will be. And it's an honor to have grown up with him as my friend.

If anything, he has taught me more about the value of life and how to live it because you are not promised tomorrow. Never stray away from your morals, and give all the Glory to God."

Edwin Evers had this to say about Derek when the story was written in the fishing magazine. "Derek was somebody you wanted to be like. He said I was his hero but in fact it turned out that Derek was my hero. I put his decal (In loving memory of Derek) on my boat in a place where I can see it, and when I struggle as an angler, and I start thinking fishing is life or death. I see the decal and I realize that it is not and I get peaceful. Derek taught me that."

While the battle with cancer was going on, Derek would get several cards a week from people all over the country. Filled with encouragement and hope, or just telling funny stories about their football glory days or fishing days.

One such card had caught my eye. It had a red bird on the front of it and red birds are special to me because of seeing one that God sent to me as a sign, on the morning that my mom passed away. The woman that wrote the card was named Sarah and she said: "I was trying to get a pizza from a local pizza place one night which happened to be the same night as a fundraiser was going on for Derek. They told me it was going to be a two and a half hour wait. I realized there was a lot of people pulling and praying for you. I wonder how many people have come to know our Lord Jesus Christ as a result of knowing you and your situation. You have made a difference in the life of family and friends, but please know you have made a difference to complete stranger's lives too. Yours in Christ, Sarah."

Jason Keniston, Derek's cousin, wanted people to know this about Derek. "Jesus is the reason my soul is eternally saved, but you are the reason I know it. When I met you for that one moment in life, I truly felt like Christ was with you. You are the most selfless, courageous, and humble person I have ever met. Because of you, I have an undying passion and love for Jesus and a servant's heart for others. I wish I had more time to tell what you meant to me but in the words of John "Though I have much to write you, I would rather not use paper and ink, Instead I hope to come to you and talk face to face so that our joy may be complete." (2nd John 12) With love, Jason

Bobby, Derek and Tyler shooting bows

Derek showing little brother Daren how to shoot a bow

Tyler and Derek catching fish

Derek and Daren fishing in the boat they worked so hard to buy.

Derek and Edwin Evers fishing.

Derek with his brothers David and Daren
starting the fight together.

CHAPTER 14

WHO AM I

Derek was born on June 25th 1990 and from the time he was born until he went home to be with the Lord, he was always full of life and adventure. He was always looking forward to something. He had a mischievous grin, and his smile was contagious and his heart was that of a warrior, yet full of love at the same time.

From a young age he had a fishing pole, or some type of ball in his hand. Derek loved fishing, playing little league baseball, and Jr. High and High school football.

He would spend hours at a fishing pond or lake with dad and his brothers or his best friend Tyler. He would be outside till dark, throwing a baseball or football around in the back yard. He also liked hunting, though he didn't get to go very often. He loved the challenge of a Bow verses a gun and would spend hours practicing in the backyard with his close friends Tyler and Bobby.

Derek's 2 favorite holidays were Christmas and the 4th of July. . He loved the huge Christmas Tree we always put up and all the lights and ornaments we would have on it. When he was younger he would turn the lights off and only have the tree lit, then he would lay under it and just look up and watch the lights dance. Every year Dad would read the Christmas Story from the Bible no matter how old the kids were, we always gathered around on Christmas Eve before bed time and read it.

One of the things we remember the most about Derek as a young boy was on Christmas Morning about 3 a.m. he would be standing by dad's bedside asking if it was time to get up and open presents yet. We would say no and send him back to bed. But he would go in the living room and lay on the couch waiting for us to get up and after a while if we still hadn't gotten up, he would have already separated all of the presents when we got up. Also when his little brother came along and was old enough he would switch and send him into our room to try and get us up early so they could open presents.

The 4th of July was always a big deal in our family. He loved all the Grilled food, watermelon, ice cold pop, homemade ice cream, and loved lighting up the sky with all kinds of fireworks. Usually he would have some friends over, and between his brothers, other family members, and friends, they would have several mortar rounds going off at the same time. Trying to make as much noise and flashes in the sky as possible. The only part that he and his brothers did not like was the next morning. Because usually everyone had left the night before and they would have to pick up tons of confetti and paper from the firework show that had fallen in our yard, and the neighbor's yard.

As he grew Derek excelled in the classroom, at sports, and fishing. Derek was not big in physical size. But his heart you could not measure. Derek was very competitive and pushed himself to do his best and work hard.

One such time was when he had pitched against a baseball team that just played better, but Derek pushed himself hard and did not give up, they still lost, but barely. After the game the other coach who had won, was so impressed by Derek and the way he handled himself, he walked up to him and gave him the game ball and told him he had the heart of a winner. As the years went by, even though his team had played and won many tournaments and won trophies and medals, that was the only ball he had kept. It still sits on his dad's dresser to this day.

When Derek played High school football, he was fast and quick as a cat. He played wide receiver and scored several touchdowns. One thing I remember, and we played it at his funeral was when he scored a touchdown, catching a beautiful pass against his cross county rivals his senior year. There was a local news team there that had caught the touchdown on film and after the touchdown he turned and saluted the camera. He wasn't being cocky or anything. It was just Derek being Derek, larger than life and loving life.

While in school he made mostly straight A's and worked at jobs to help pay for his insurance and phone bill, and was also saving to get a bass boat to someday be in a bass fishing league with his best friend Tyler who was also hooked on fishing.

During the summer Derek worked as a little league umpire along with his other job. He said he liked umpiring and helping the kids when he could with pointers on hitting or fielding as he was working.

The loves in his life were his mom, dad, brothers, girlfriend and his faithful golden retriever Missy, which he had went and bought himself with his own money when he was 16.

Derek was saved at the age of 13 and he was active in Church and was a firm believer in Christ. We were told about several times when he had witnessed to friends and others.

He had went to college to study to become a radiologist, but his dream was to become a Professional Bass Fisherman. He had always said it would be nice to do something you love and help someone along the way as he did it. After his freshman year in College, Derek was able to get a used bass boat and he and Tyler entered a small Bass fishing League that would have some weekend tournaments. They were also trying to get the college to start up a chapter for a college bass fishing team that other colleges had already been doing. They had to write up by laws and get it all approved before they could ever get the chapter going. This was the beginning of his sophomore year. At that time was when we found Derek's Cancer. He had to pull out of school and everything was put on hold.

When Derek was diagnosed with cancer he met it head on and never complained. Knowing he had the support and prayers of his home town behind him, Saying *"I have faith in God and know that His plan is perfect– whatever happens, I know that He can bring good from anything, even this."* He also said **"WHO AM I** IF God needs to do his work in this way?" When he was asked how he felt about having cancer. Here as a 19 year old young man wiser in years than most of us and yet he faced it head on.

Derek wrote in his journal only a few times as his time was coming to an end and this is what he said:

8-20-2010

Today I shot my bow. I was a little rusty. Today I started a journal. I feel good about it. I read out of the bible. I really feel this will help me get closer to our Father. I really want to feel His presence and feel his touch in my life. I love James and Tonya, they are awesome. They are truly amazing people. (They were Derek's college and career leaders At First Baptist where we attended, who came to our home every week, because of Derek's immune system being so low he was not able to get out in public much. So they would come over and we would have what was called Keniston Night. They would have a bible study with all of us. There were also times when Derek could not get out of bed due to the chemo he had just had, but they would come over anyway, and just visit and love on us and Derek and would always pray with us before leaving.

41

They brought comfort and love to us during a very hard time. You knew they were not doing it out of any obligation but out of love for us.) I love my family. I am working on being a better brother to Daren. I know how much I looked up to my older brother David, so I'm going try to start being better to Daren. I really do love you bro. Well going to bed. Big day tomorrow. Love all you guys.

08-22-2010

Yesterday was awesome! Me and my girlfriend took a road trip to Bass Pro in Springfield, Mo. It was so fun. I love spending time with her. Anyway we read 5 chapters in the Bible but I fell asleep before I was able to wright so I am writing today. If I am being honest I'm not feeling so great anymore. I feel like I'm getting closer to death every day. I hate it. Not gonna lie, it scares me. I don't wanna die young. There's so much I wanna still do. But if it is God's will that He brings me home to heal me, I understand. But I would really like to be healed here on earth.

I'm not gonna give up, I'm gonna keep praying. But I wish something significant would happen so I would kinda have an idea which way it's leaning toward. I really think it's getting closer and closer for it to be my time to be with grandma, and grandpa. As much as I hate to think about it. I really have that gut feeling, my time is close. Could be tomorrow, could be weeks or months, but I don't have a good feeling.

So if something happens before I get to write again, just know, I Love All you guys. Mom, Dad, David, Daren, Kelsea, and Missy, and all my other family and friends. I love everyone so much. I will miss you, but I really believe I will see you all again. Which will be a glorious day. Anyway, I love you all. Goodnight.

-Derek

THE THANK
YOU PRAYER

Father God in heaven, first off I want to thank you for getting us
through this. We want to remember and thank so many people
who were with us through this. Our Church Family First Baptist
Claremore, and all of the other Church Congregations in our
community, and all of the wonderful people who were there and
helped in so many ways. From bringing us dinners each night,
hugging us, praying with us and for loving us. For our Pastor and
staff, The Doctors and staff at the Cancer center, and the hospital
who blessed us with their hearts as they helped our family. The
Catch a Dream Foundation, All the cards of encouragement and
stories from around the country and some across the other side of
the world. For Uncles, and For Aunts who gave of themselves and
was willing to help wherever needed, and a Grandmothers love
who was always near. For Best Friends who stayed by Derek's
side till the end. For our Rocks of support that we leaned on, who
would come over, who cried with us, held our hands, pray with us
and just love on us. For countless prayers offered up on peoples
knees, and the support of a community who rallied around with
fundraisers, prayers, and kind words for one of their own. For
Teachers, Coaches, and Sunday School Teachers, who helped us
raise such a wonderful young man. We thank you Father for the
wonderful 20 years we got to spend with Derek. For choosing us

to be his parents and raise him, and take care of him until you called him home. Father I pray that you will bless all of the above people and if Derek could tell them thank you personally he would, and will someday. In Jesus name. Amen.

"IT'S NOT HOW YOU DIE, IT'S HOW YOU LIVE!"

"Derek Keniston"

Derek's Biggest Bass!

Printed in the United States
By Bookmasters